English Code 1

Activity Book

Progress Chart

You did it!	Well done!	Fantastic!	Super!

Unit 8

Unit 7

Unit 6

Unit 5

Unit 4

Unit 3

Unit 2

Unit 1

Creativity	Critical thinking	Coding	Communication

Contents

Welcome!

How can I have fun at school?

1 002 Listen and number. Then write.

bag   book   chair   door   pencil   table   window

2 Cover a photo in 1. Play *What's missing?*

Book!

Yes!

3 003 Listen to the song. Then greet your partner.

Hello, how are you?

I'm great, thank you.

I'm OK, thanks.

How about you?

My colourful classroom

I will learn colour words and number words **1–10**.

1 🎧 004 **Listen and complete in the correct colour.**

1 ___ed **2** ___ink **3** ___reen **4** ___range **5** ___lack

6 ___urple **7** ___rown **8** ___lue **9** ___ellow

2 Look and colour. Then say the colours and numbers.

3 💡 **Look at 2. Which numbers from 0–10 are missing?**

MATHS ZONE

4 Read and draw.

7 purple books

4 pink chairs

I can use colour words and number words 1–10.

Language lab

GRAMMAR: OPEN YOUR BOOK

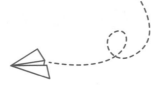

I will learn how to follow instructions in English.

1 Listen and continue the sequence.

CODE CRACKER

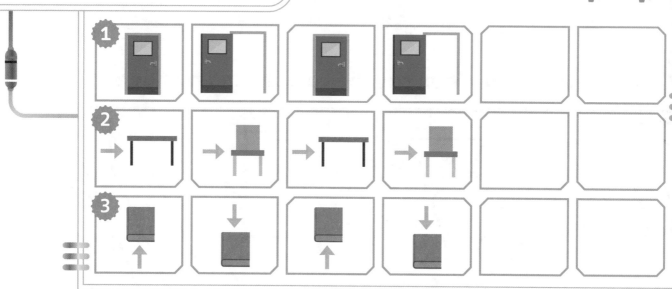

2 Read and match.

1 Open your book. •
2 Pick up your pencil. •
3 Stand up. •
4 Open the window. •
5 Pick up your bag. •

• Put down your pencil.
• Put down your bag.
• Shut your book.
• Sit down.
• Shut the window.

3 Play *Opposites tennis*.

Open the door!

Shut the door!

I can follow instructions in English.

Story lab

I will read a story and learn how to introduce myself.

Hello!

1 Read the story again. Then complete.

1 Hi! I'm _____ . I'm _____ .

Hello! My name is _____ .
I'm _____ .

2 Here's _____ ! She's _____ .

Hello!

2 Read and match. Then ask and answer.

8 •

4 •

9 •

2 •

• N-I-N-E

• E-I-G-H-T

• T-W-O

• F-O-U-R

How do you spell 8?

E-I-G-H-T

3 Order and write the questions. Then ask and answer.

1 you? are How   _____

2 What's name? your   _____

3 do How spell that? you   _____

4 old you? How are   _____

I can read a story and learn how to introduce myself.

1 Let's play!

How can I make a toy that floats?

1 🎧 006 Listen to the song and number.

CODE CRACKER

2 💡 Circle and say. Then tick ☑ what is missing from the song.

1  ⬜
aeroplane / train

2  ⬜
car / boat

3  ⬜
aeroplane / boat

4  ⬜
train / car

Go aeroplane!

3 Which car gets to school first? Count the blocks and circle.

MATHS ZONE

The blue / yellow / red car gets to school first.

Toy room

I will learn toy words.

1 Find and circle 10 toys.

buscardollballtrainoctopusaeroplanebuildingblocksboatteddybear

2 Look and write.

EXTRA VOCABULARY

3 007 Read, listen and tick ☑. Then colour.

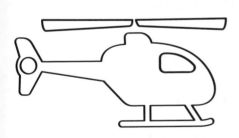

a red helicopter ☐

a blue car ☐

a green van ☐

a red aeroplane ☐

a blue motorbike ☐

a green bus ☐

I can use toy words.

Language lab 1

GRAMMAR 1: IT'S A / AN ...

I will name toy words using **It's a / It's an.**

1 Read and match.

1 I am   2 It is   3 What is   4 He is   5 She is

What's   It's   He's   She's   I'm

2 Look and complete.

1 What's this?

It's _a teddy bear_ .

2 What's this?

It's _____ ball.

3 What's this?

_____ an aeroplane.

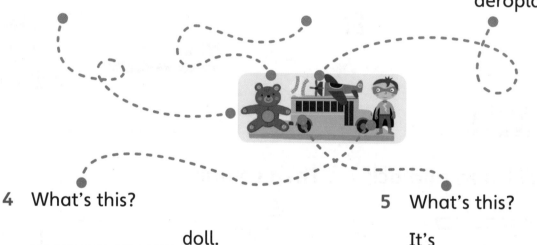

4 What's this?

_____ doll.

5 What's this?

It's _____ .

3 Make a toy silhouette. Then ask and answer.

What's this?

It's a doll.

I can name toy words using It's a / It's an ... .

Story lab

I will read a story about toys.

Let's play together

1 ⚙ **Make your story book.** ➡ page 97

1 Order and write the page numbers.

2 Complete the story.

3 Draw a cover.

4 Complete the story review.

2 **Look and complete.**

1 What's this?

It's _____ .

2 What's this?

It's _____ .

3 What's this?

It's _____ .

3 ⚙ **Make a toy from a box.**
Then ask and answer.

What's this?

It's a car.

I can read a story about toys.

Phonics lab

I will learn the **p** and **b** sounds.

1 008 **Look, listen and circle p or b. Then say.**

Colour me!

1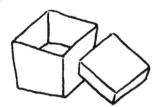

p
b
ox

2

p
b
ed

3

p
b
en

4

p
b
anda

2 Write the missing letters. Then say.

The _____anda has got a _____en and a _____encil.

3 009 **Listen and write the missing letters. Then read and colour.**

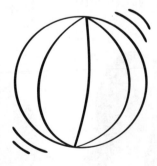

1 What's this?
It's a _____lue _____all.

2 What's this?
It's a _____urple _____arrot.

I can use the **p** and **b** sounds.

I will learn about toy materials.

1 **Look and write.**

fabric   metal
plastic   wood

1 It's an _____ .
It's made of _____ .

2 It's a _____ _____ .
It's made of _____ .

3 It's a _____ .
It's made of _____ .

4 It's a _____ .
It's made of _____ .

EXPERIMENT TIME

Report

1 **Complete the table.**

Toy	Material	Float	Sink

2 **Write your report.**

Float or sink?

It's a boat. It's made of plastic. It floats.

Float or sink?

It's _____ . It's made of
_____ . It _____ .

I **know** about toy materials.

Language lab 2

GRAMMAR 2: IT'S A BIG / SMALL ...

I will describe toys.

1 ⚙ Look, read and number.

1 It's a black building block.

2 It's a small building block.

3 It's a blue building block.

4 It's a big building block.

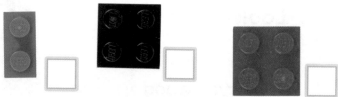

2 Order and write. Then look and write T (True) or F (False).

CODE CRACKER ⚙⚙⚙

1 big   It's   bear.   teddy   a

_____

2 ball.   It's   big   a

_____

3 a   car.   small   It's

_____

4 red   a   It's   aeroplane.

_____

3 Look at 2. Correct the false sentences.

1 _____

2 _____

I can describe toys.

14

I know!

I will ask and answer about objects.

1 🎧 010 **Listen and say
I know or I don't know.**

I don't know.

2 🎧 011 **Look, listen and tick ☑ .**

3 💡 **Ask and answer. Then complete.**

What's this?

I don't know.

I know! It's an aeroplane.

It's _____ . It's _____ . It's _____ .

I can ask and answer about objects.

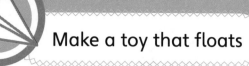

Make a toy that floats

Project report

1 Tick ☑ for your toy.

Type of toy

| bus ☐ | car ☐ | aeroplane ☐ | boat ☐ | train ☐ |

| doll ☐ | ball ☐ | teddy bear ☐ | octopus ☐ |

building blocks ☐   _____ ☐

Size	**Material**
big ☐ small ☐	paper ☐ metal ☐
Float or sink?	fabric ☐ plastic ☐
float ☐ sink ☐	wood ☐

2 Complete your project report.

My toy boat

It's a paper boat.
It's orange.
It's small.
It floats!

My toy _____
It's a _____ .
It's _____ .
It's big / small .
It floats / sinks .

I can make a toy that floats.

3 Present your report to your family and friends.

This is my toy boat. It's made of paper.

4 Read, look and number.

1 It's made of fabric.

2 It's made of wood.

3 It's a big toy.

4 It's a small toy.

5 It floats.

6 It sinks.

5 Look at 4. Ask and answer.

What's this?

It's a small train.

6 Read and write. Then complete a clue for your partner.

It's small.
It's plastic.
It's red.
It's _____ .

It's _____ .
It's _____ .
It's _____ .
It's a/an _____ .

Now go to your Progress Chart on page 2.

2 Art club!

How can I make an art shop?

1 🎧 012 Listen to the song and colour in order.

CODE CRACKER

2 Read and write the numbers.

MATHS ZONE

1 four red crayons + two blue crayons

$\boxed{4}$ + $\boxed{2}$ =

$\boxed{6}$ crayons

2 two green colouring pens + one pink colouring pen $\boxed{}$ + $\boxed{}$ =

$\boxed{}$ colouring pens

3 five orange colouring pencils + three yellow colouring pencils

$\boxed{}$ + $\boxed{}$ =

$\boxed{}$ colouring pencils

3 💡 Match, write and say.

1

_____

Red crayon!

2

_____

3

_____

What do we need?

I will learn art item words.

1 Write the words.

1 p c e o n l c o i u l r s i h n a g r p p e e n n c e i r l

pencil sharpener   _colouring pencil_

2 r c u r b a b y e o r n

_____ _____

3 p p e a n i c n i t l b c r a u s s e h

_____ _____

2 Look and write.

1 _____ 2 _____ 3 _____ 4 _____ 5 _____

6 _____ 7 _____ 8 _____ 9 _____ 10 _____

3 [013] Look, listen and match. Then ask and answer.

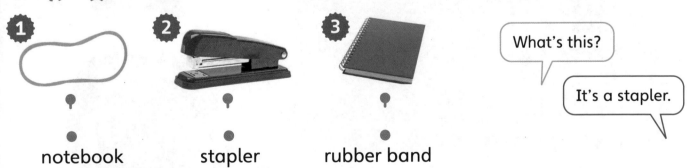

notebook   stapler   rubber band

What's this?

It's a stapler.

I can use art item words.

Language lab 1

GRAMMAR 1: THERE'S / ARE ...

I will learn to count using **There's / There are.**

1 Read and circle.

1 (There's) / There are two colouring pens.   2   There's / There are a paint pot

3 (There's) / There are a pencil case.   4   There's / There are four glue sticks

2 Look and complete. Then write T (True) or F (False).

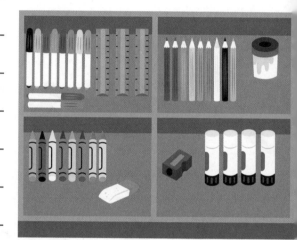

1 _There are_ ten colouring pens   _T_

2 _____ three rulers.   ___

3 _____ one colouring pencil.   ___

4 _____ a paint pot.   ___

5 _____ nine crayons.   ___

6 _____ a rubber.   ___

7 _____ a pencil sharpener.   ___

8 _____ three glue sticks.   ___

3 Count the items in your pencil case. Then tell your partner.

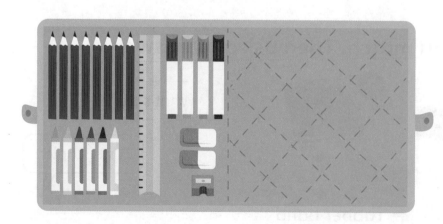

There are four colouring pens.

I can count art items using There's / There are .

Story lab

I will read a story about the playhouse.

A rainbow playhouse

1 Make your story book. → page 99

1 Order and write the page numbers.
2 Complete the story.
3 Draw a cover.
4 Complete the story review.

2 Look and complete.

1 There's blue, yellow and _____ paint.

2 There's orange, blue and _____ paint.

3 There's blue, red and _____ paint.

3 Design your own playhouse. Then say.

There's a small table.

I can read a story about the playhouse.

Phonics lab

I will learn the **d** and **t** sounds.

1 Look, listen and circle d or t. Then say.

1 The
d
t
uck talks to the
d
t
iger.

2 The
d
t
ortoise is named
D
T
aisy.

2 Write d or t. Then say.

Colour me!

1 _____able

2 _____oor

3 _____en

3 Listen and write the missing letters. Then read and draw.

1 There are _____en _____eddy bears.

2 There's a _____og and a _____oll.

I can use the **d** and **t** sounds.

I will learn about mixing colours.

1 Look and label. Then circle *P* for primary colours or *S* for secondary colours.

blue   green   orange   purple   red   yellow

1 _____
P / S

3 _____
P / S

5 _____
P / S

2 _____
P / S

4 _____
P / S

6 _____
P / S

EXPERIMENT TIME

Report

1 Complete the table.

Colour 1	Colour 2	Result

2 Write your report.

Dark and light colours

red + white = pink
It's a light colour.

How can I make dark and light colours?

red + white = _____
It's a **light** / dark colour.

red + green = _____
It's a light / **dark** colour.

black + white = _____
It's a **light** / dark colour.

I know about mixing colours.

Language lab 2

GRAMMAR 2: HOW MANY ...?

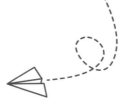

I will ask about art items using How many ...?

1 Read and match.

1   How many rubbers are there? •

2   How many paint pots are there? •

3   How many pencil cases are there? •

• There are three paint pots.

• There's one pencil case.

• There are five rubbers.

2 Order and write. Then complete.

CODE CRACKER

1   there?   paint   How   are   pots   many

_____

There are _____ paint pots.

2   many   there?   How   are   colouring pens

_____

There _____ colouring pens.

3   sharpeners   How   pencil   there?   are   many

_____

_____ pencil sharpener.

3 Guess the number of building blocks. Then check with your partner.

MATHS ZONE

How many yellow building blocks are there?

There are seven yellow building blocks.

I can ask about art items using How many ...?

Being polite

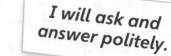
I will ask and answer politely.

1 🎧 016 **Listen and number. Then say.**

Thank you. ☐

Here you are. ☐

Two paintbrushes, please. ☐

2 🎧 017 **Listen and draw 😃 or 🙁.**

1 ◯

2 ◯

3 ◯

3 💬 **Role-play a toy shop.**

Two balls, please.

Here you are.

Thank you.

I can ask and answer about items politely.

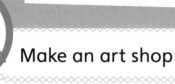 Make an art shop

Project report

1 Complete for your art shop.

Art item	Number
rulers	
colouring pens	
colouring pencils	
crayons	
paint pots	
glue sticks	
rubbers	
pencil sharpeners	
paintbrushes	
pencil cases	

2 Complete your project report.

My art shop

There are four colouring pens.
There are five rulers.
There are seven rubbers.
There's one pencil case.

My art shop

There's / There are _____ .
There's / There are _____ .
There's / There are _____ .
There's / There are _____ .

I can make an art shop.

3 Present your report to your family and friends.

This is my art shop. There are four colouring pens.

4 Count and write.

colouring pencils ☐

paint pots ☐

glue sticks ☐

crayons ☐

rubbers ☐

colouring pens ☐

5 Look at 4. Ask and answer.

How many rulers are there?

There are three rulers.

6 Read and circle. Then complete.

Primary / Secondary **colours**	Primary / Secondary **colours**
_____ three blue rulers.	There's one green _____ .
There's one red _____ .	There are two _____ colouring pens.
There are _____ yellow rubbers.	_____ one orange pencil sharpener.

Now go to your Progress Chart on page 2.

1 Checkpoint

1 Read and match.

1 pencil   2 teddy   3 paint   4 building   5 glue

bear   blocks   stick   sharpener   pot

2 Draw a path and colour.

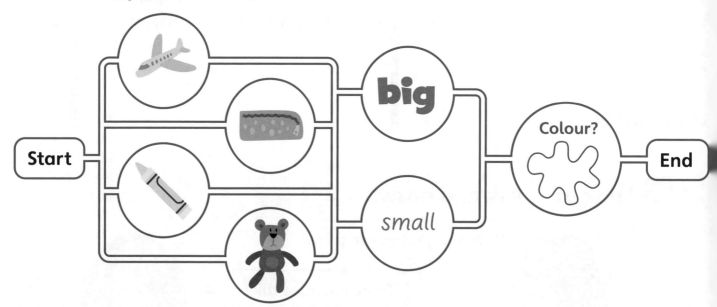

3 Look at 2. Complete and draw.

1 What's this?   It's a / an _____ .

2 Is it big or small?   It's _____ .

3 What colour is it?   It's _____ .

4 How many _____ are there in your class?

There is / are _____ _____ .

Crafts around the world

1 Look, read and circle.

1 It's a bag / book.

2 It's an aeroplane / octopus.

3 It's a bus / car.

4 It's a llama / teddy bear.

2 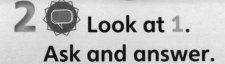 Look at **1**. Ask and answer.

 What's this?

It's origami! It's a book.

3 Count, circle and write. Then check with your partner.

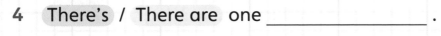
aeroplane   dolls   glue stick   paintbrushes   paint pots   rulers

1   There's / There are eight _____ .

2   There's / There are nine _____ .

3   There's / There are four _____ .

4   There's / There are one _____ .

5   There's / There are two _____ .

6   There's / There are one _____ .

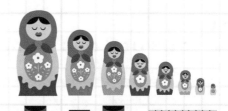

How many dolls are there?

There are eight dolls.

3 Families

How can I make a family decoration?

1 018 **Listen to the song. Choose and write words to make a new chorus.**

1 dad   mum   baby

2 happy   small   great

2 Look and write.

baby   dad   mum

Family 1

Family 2

3 Look at 2 and complete.

MATHS ZONE

Family 1   There are ☐ people.

Family 2   There are ☐ people.

1   Which family is big?
Family _____ is _____ .

2   Which family is small?
_____

Welcome to my family

VOCABULARY

I will learn family words.

1 Complete the family words.

ad (2)   by   cle   ma   nt   um   sin   ter   ther

1 grand___ma___   2 d_____   3 bro_____   4 grand_____

5 m_____   6 ba_____   7 sis_____   8 un_____

9 au_____   10 cou_____

2 Look and write.

7 _____

8 _____

__grandma__

2 _____

3 _____

4 _____

5 _____

6 _____

9 _____

10 _____

EXTRA VOCABULARY

3 Look, listen and match. Then count and say.

1 triplets   2 only child   3 twins

How many children are there?

There are three brothers. They're triplets.

I can use family words.

31

Language lab 1

GRAMMAR 1: THIS IS MY / YOUR / HIS / HER

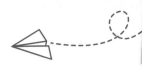

I will introduce my family using **This is**.

1 Follow and complete.

1 _____This_____ is me.

2 This _____ my brother.

3 This is _____ sister.

This is _____ football.

This is ___my___ teddy bear.

This is _____ train.

2 Draw you and your partner with toys. Then complete.

This is me. This is _____ .

This is you. This is _____ .

3 Make family bookmarks. Tell your partner.

grandma

This is your grandma!

Yes! This is my grandma. This is her bookmark.

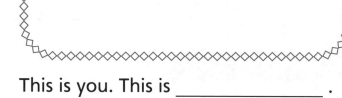

I can introduce my family using This is .

Story lab

I will read a story about family.

My BIG family

1 ⚙ Make your story book. ➡ page 101

1 Order and write the page numbers.

2 Complete the story.

3 Draw a cover.

4 Complete the story review.

2 Look and circle Alexander's family. Then write about them.

1 This is _____ _____ , Sarah.

2 This _____ _____ mum.

3 This is _____ _____ .

3 ⚙ Draw a party at your house. Then say.

This is my aunt.

I can read a story about family.

Phonics lab

1 🔊 020 Look, listen and write g or k.

1 ____ing   **2** ____ite   **3** ____irl   **4** ____ame

2 Complete with the words in 1. Then say.

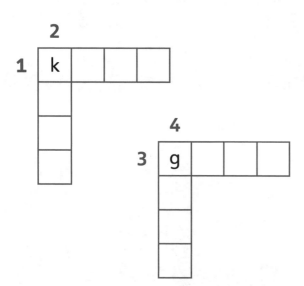

3 🔊 021 Listen and write the missing letters. Then say.

1 The ____irl has got a ____ite.

2 The ____ing plays a ____ame.

3 The ____irl likes the ____ing.

4 Look, draw and write.

_____

I can use the **g** and **k** sounds.

I will learn about shapes.

1. How many sides? Count.

MATHS ZONE

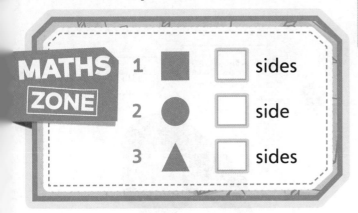

1 ⬛ ☐ sides

2 ⬤ ☐ side

3 ▲ ☐ sides

2. Colour the picture. Then count the shapes and say.

EXPERIMENT TIME

Report

1 Complete the table.

My jigsaw	
Family	**Shapes**

2 Write your report.

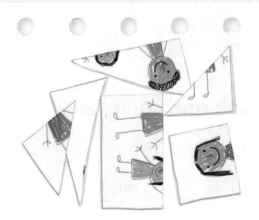

My family jigsaw

This is my mum, my dad and me.

There are four triangles in my jigsaw.

My family jigsaw

This is _____.

There are _____

in my jigsaw.

I know about shapes.

Language lab 2

GRAMMAR 2: WHO ...?

1 ⚙ Ask and answer. Then colour and check.

1

Who's this?

This is his ...

2

Who's this?

This is her ...

2 Look and complete.

1 Who's this? _____ his mum.

2 _____ this? This is _____ .

3 Who's _____ ? This _____ .

3 🔲 Play *Reveal.*

Who's this?

This is your brother!

I can ask about family using Who's this?

Making new friends

COMMUNICATION

I will introduce my friends.

1 Listen and number.

Nuan

Amin

Samira

2 Read and circle the differences. Then act out.

1 Hello! I'm Samantha.

Hi! I'm Oliver.

2 Nice to meet you, Oliver.

Nice to meet you, Samantha.

CODE CRACKER

Hi! I'm Leo.

Hello! I'm Ana.

Nice to meet you, Ana.

Nice to meet you, Leo.

3 Draw finger friends. Role-play making new friends.

Hello! I'm Hugo. Who are you?

Hi! I'm Charlotte. This is my friend Ayesha.

Nice to meet you, Hugo.

I can introduce my friends.

Create a family playhouse decoration

Project report

1 Complete for your decoration. Write your family members and colour.

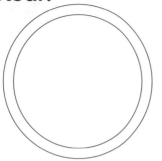

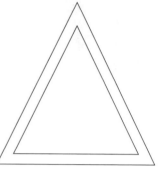

_____   _____   _____

2 Complete your project report.

My grandma
Rosa

My grandma
Ana

My grandad
Carlos

My mum   My dad   My aunt
Tania   My uncle
Ricardo

My brother
Diego

Me

Baby Andrea

My family playhouse decoration

This is my family playhouse decoration.
Look! There's a triangle. This is my
grandma, Rosa.
There's a square. This is my mum.
There's a circle. This is my brother, Diego.

My family playhouse decoration

This is my family playhouse decoration.
Look! There's a _____ .
This is my _____ .
There's a _____ .
This _____ .

I can make a family decoration.

3 💬 Present your report to your family and friends.

This is my family decoration. There are three triangles. This is my grandma, Rosa.

4 Look and circle Ana's family.

1 (mum) / uncle   2 (baby) / aunt

3 (brother) / dad   4 grandad / (brother)

5 💬 Look at 4. Ask and answer.

Who's this?

This is her mum.

6 💡 Read and complete.

You: Hello! I'm _____ .

Ana: Hi! I'm Ana. Nice to _____ you.

You: _____ to meet you, too, Ana.

Ana: _____ this?

You: _____ is my friend, _____ .

Ana: Hello, _____ .

4 Puppet show!

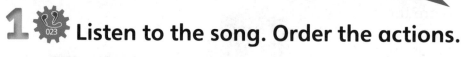

How can I do a puppet show?

1 🎧 023 **Listen to the song. Order the actions.**

 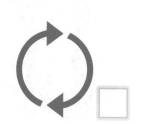  

2 Look and write.

> hands   head   leg

1 _____

2 _____

3 _____

3 Look and do the actions. Then draw your own routine and say.

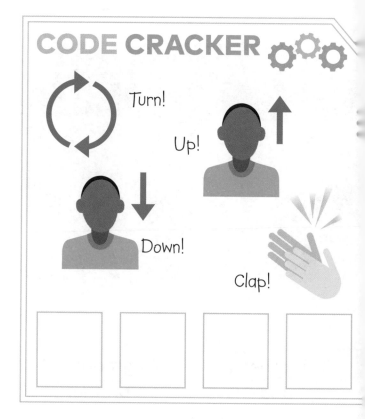

CODE CRACKER

Turn!

Up!

Down!

Clap!

My body

I will learn body words.

1 Complete the crossword.

arms   ears   eyes   face   feet   hair
hands   head   legs   mouth   nose

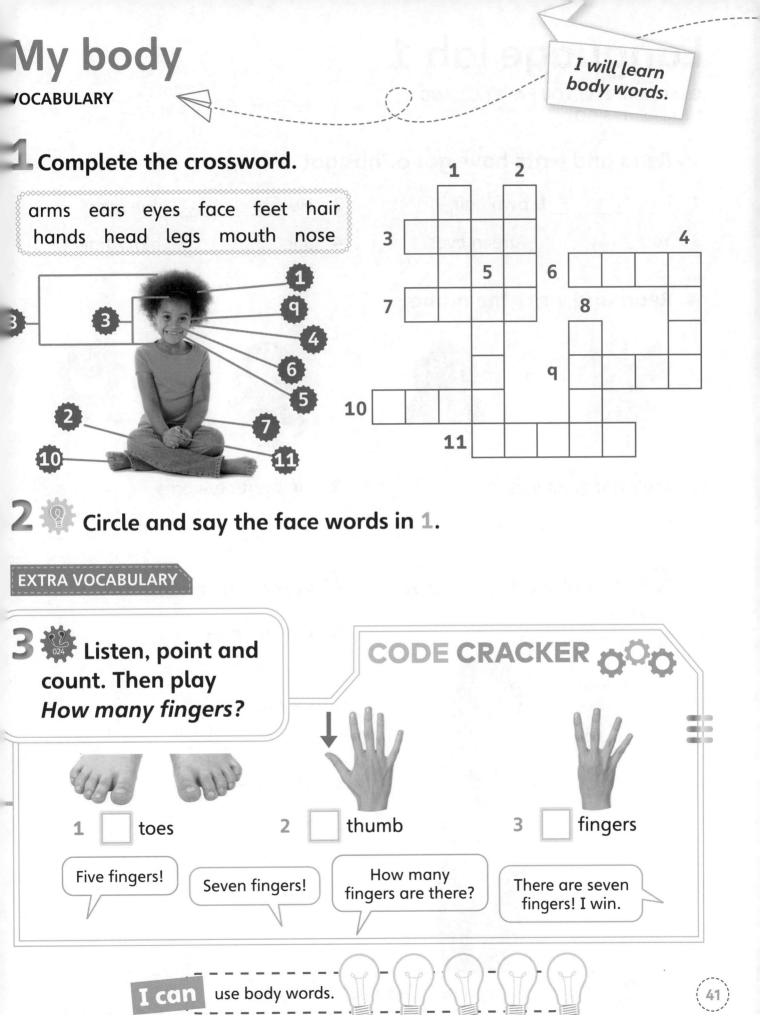

2 Circle and say the face words in **1**.

3 024 Listen, point and count. Then play *How many fingers?*

CODE CRACKER

1 ☐ toes   2 ☐ thumb   3 ☐ fingers

Five fingers!

Seven fingers!

How many fingers are there?

There are seven fingers! I win.

I can use body words.

Language lab 1

GRAMMAR 1: I / YOU HAVE GOT AND HE / SHE HAS GOT

*I will describe people using **have got / has got**.*

1 Read and write have got or has got.

1 I _____ brown hair.

2 He _____ blue eyes.

3 You _____ green eyes.

4 She _____ black hair.

2 Read and write the name.

Ed

Olivia

Jilly

Leo

1 She's got eight legs. _____

2 He's got blue ears. _____

3 He's got a brown nose. _____

4 She's got orange hair. _____

3  Describe a toy to your partner.

This is my teddy bear. He's got two brown ears.

4 Write sentences.

1 I / two / ears

   I _ve got two ears_____.

2 He / two / legs

   He _____.

3 She / one / nose

   She _____.

4 You / two / hands

   You _____.

I can describe people using have got / has got .

Story lab

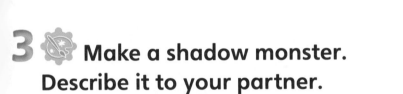

I will read a story about a monster.

It's a monster!

1 Make your story book. ➔ page 103

1 Order and write the page numbers.

2 Complete the story.

3 Draw a cover and what happens next.

4 Complete the story review.

2 Write about the shadow.

1 It _____ big ears.

2 It's got six _____ .

3 It _____ three _____ .

3 Make a shadow monster. Describe it to your partner.

It's got a big mouth.

I can read a story about a monster.

Phonics lab

I will learn the **z** and **s** sounds.

1 Colour **z** red **and** s blue.

Colour me!

2 **Listen and circle. Then say.**

The sad zebra / sister sits in the zoo / sun .

3 Write **z** or **s** and say.

1 ____un

2 ____oo

3 ____ing

4 ____ebra

I can use the **z** and **s** sounds.

44

I will learn about the five senses.

1 Look and write. Then draw.

hear   see   smell   taste   touch

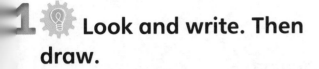

1 I _____ with my hands.

2 I _____ with my mouth.

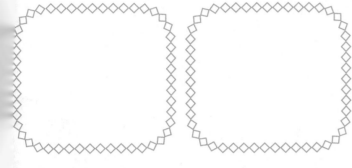

3 I _____ with my eyes.

4 I _____ with my nose.

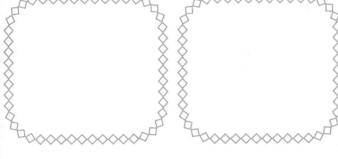

5 I _____ with my ears.

I know about the five senses.

EXPERIMENT TIME

Report

1 Complete the table.

Can I guess the taste?		
	My guess	**Result**
Food 1		
Food 2		

2 Write your report.

Can I guess the taste?

Food 1

My guess: It's chocolate.

Result: Yes! It's chocolate!

Can I guess the taste?

Food 1

My guess: It's _____ .

Result: Yes / No
It's _____ .

Food 2

My guess: _____

Result: Yes / No
_____

Language lab 2

GRAMMAR 2: I'M / YOU'RE / HE'S / SHE'S

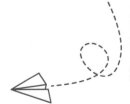

I will describe height using **I'm / You're / He's / She's**.

1 Look and write.

1 I am = ___I'm___

2 You are = _____

3 He is = _____

4 She is = _____

2 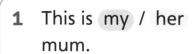 Look, read and circle.

1 This is my / her mum.

He's / She's tall.

I'm / You're short.

2 This is my / your brother.

He's / She's tall.

I'm / You're short.

3 026 Listen and write. Then measure and write about you and your partner.

CODE CRACKER

1 [l] . [2] metres tall

2 [ ] . [ ] metres tall

3 [ ] . [ ] metres tall

4 [ ] . [ ] metres tall

I'm [ ] . [ ] metres tall.

My partner is [ ] . [ ] metres tall.

I can  describe height using I'm / You're / He's / She's .

What a big teddy bear!

I will talk about surprising things.

1 Look, listen and write.

big   small   short   tall

1   What a _____ boat!

3   What a _____ girl!

2   What a _____ boat!

4   What a _____ girl!

2 Use and to complete the sentences. Then use and to describe your partner.

You're tall and you've got black hair.

CODE CRACKER

1   He's short. His dad is tall.

He's short ___and his dad___
_____ .

2   She's short. Her sister is tall.

She's short _____
_____ .

I can talk about surprising things.

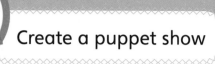

Create a puppet show

1 Complete for your puppet and your partner's puppet.

	My puppet	My partner's puppet
Name		
Size		
Body parts		

2 Complete your project report.

My puppet

This is *my puppet*. Her name is Big Bug. She's got three eyes. She's got six legs. She's small.

Our puppet show

This is *my puppet*. _____
name is _____ . _____'s
got _____ _____ and she's /
he's _____ .
This is *my partner's puppet*. _____
name is _____ . _____'s
got _____ _____ and
she's / he's _____ .

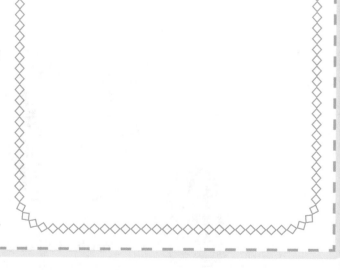

I can do a puppet show.

3 💬 **Present your report to your family and friends.**

This is my puppet. Her name is Big Bug. She's got a green face!

4 Look, read and write the name.

 Uncle Bob

 Mrs Bag

 Pinocchio

 Aunt Moo

 Ribbit

 Mary-Jo

1 He's got a big nose. _____

3 He's got big eyes. _____

5 She's got a small, green nose. _____

2 She's got small feet. _____

4 She's small. _____

6 He's got a big, red mouth _____

5 💬 **Look at 4. Point and tell your partner something surprising.**

What big eyes!

6 Read and complete. Then write a clue for your partner.

He's got two eyes.
He's got a red mouth.
He's got small hands.
He's big.
His name is _____.

He's / She's got _____.
He's / She's got _____.
He's / She's got _____.
He's / She's _____.
His / Her name is _____.

Now go to your Progress Chart on page 2.

2 Checkpoint

1 💡 Circle the odd one out.

1 mum   aunt   cousin   face   2 arms   nose   feet   uncle

3 short   grandad   tall   big   4 grandma   baby   sister   tall

2 Draw a path and colour.

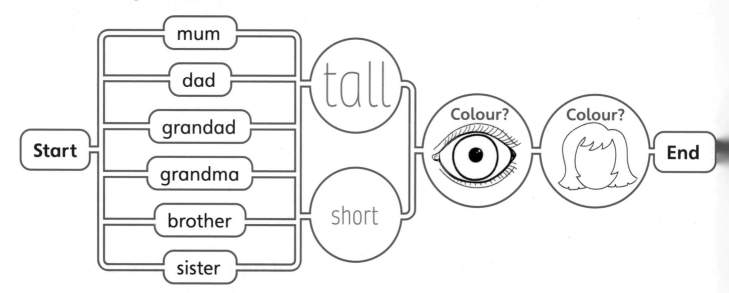

3 Look at 2. Complete and draw.

1 Who's this?

   This is _____ _____ .

2 Tall or short?

   He / She is _____ .

3 Eye colour?

   He's / She's got _____ _____ .

4 Hair colour?

   He's / She's got _____ _____ .

Let's celebrate

1 Look and colour.

1	red	2	pink
3	blue	4	purple
5	green	6	orange
7	yellow		

2 Read and complete.

brother   China   dragon   hair   head   lantern

1 This is New Year in _____ .

2 This is her _____ . He's got black _____ .

3 This is a red _____ .

4 This is a Chinese _____ . It's got a yellow and green _____ .

3 Play *Guess the New Year Festival.*

There are tall puppets.

It's New Year in Ecuador!

Yes!

5 The perfect pet

How can we choose the perfect class pet?

1 028 **Listen to the song. Then match.**

1 Woof! ●   2 Neigh! ●   3 Croak! ●

● horse   ● frog   ● dog

2 **Look and complete.**

1 What's this?

It's a _____ .

2 What's this?

It's _____ .

3 What's this?

_____

3 Read and cross ☒ the false sentences.

CODE CRACKER

1

It's small.   ☐
It's got four eyes. ☐
It's got four legs. ☐
It's yellow.   ☐

2

It's small.   ☐
It's got two ears.   ☐
It's got three legs. ☐
It's brown.   ☐

Animals around us

VOCABULARY

I will learn pet words.

1 Complete the puzzle. There are two extra words.

bird cat dog fish frog hamster horse lizard mouse rabbit

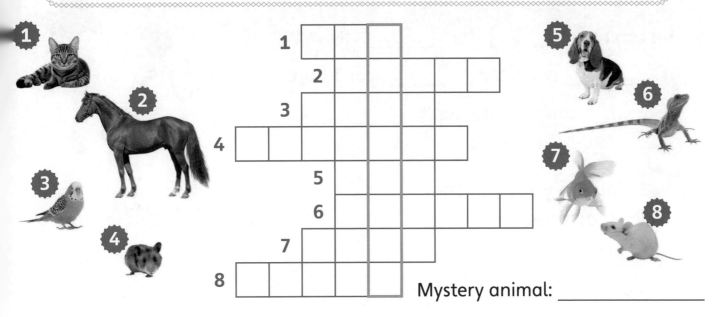

Mystery animal: _____

2 Look at 1. Write the two missing animals.

_____   _____

EXTRA VOCABULARY

3 Look, listen and number. Then ask and answer.

It's got eight legs. It's black and brown.

It's a spider!

☐ spider   ☐ tortoise   ☐ stick insect

Language lab 1

GRAMMAR 1: I / YOU / HE / SHE CAN / CAN'T

*I will talk about actions using **can** and **can't**.*

1 Read and complete. Then match.

but can can't It it swim

1 He can run, _____ he _____ fly. •—

2 It _____ swim, but _____ can't hop. •—

3 _____ can fly, but it can't _____ . •—

2 🔊 Talk to your partner. Tick ☑ or cross ☒.

CODE CRACKER

hop	clap	swim	sing	climb	fly

I can hop, but I can't fly!

OK. You can hop, but you can't fly.

3 Write about your partner. Use the information in 2.

He / She / can / can't _____ , but _____ .

_____

I can talk about actions using can and can't .

Story lab

I will read a story about a hat.

My hat can hop!

1 ✷ Make your story book. ➡ page 105

1 Order and write the page numbers.

2 Complete the story.

3 Draw a cover.

4 Complete the story review.

2 Read and match. There is one extra sentence.

My hat can fly! ●

It can hop! ●

Look! It's a horse! ●

Sarah, your hat can swim! ●

Look! It can climb! ●

3 Write about the frog in the story.

The frog _____ green.

It's got _____ legs.

It can _____ , but it can't _____ .

It can _____ , but _____ .

 read a story about a hat.

Phonics lab

*I will learn the **m** and **n** sounds.*

1 030 Look, listen and write **m** or **n**.

1 _____um

2 _____ine

3 _____ose

4 _____ouse

2 Help the mouse to find the nut. Follow and say **m** or **n**.

3 Write the missing letters.

_____y _____ame's Nancy. What's your _____ame?

_____y _____ame's Mark.

4 Look at 3. Ask and answer with your own names.

I can use the **m** and **n** sounds.

I will learn about animal and plant needs.

1 💡 **What does a cat need to live? Tick ☑ and say.**

1

2

3

4

5

EXPERIMENT TIME

Report

1 Circle the materials you used. Then colour the correct flower.

white flower   red flower   pot

insects   water   food dye

Step 1

Step 2

2 Write your report.

Equipment	Results
white flower	Step 1: The flower is white.
pot	Step 2: The flower drinks the water and food dye. The flower is red.
water	
food dye	

Equipment	Results
_____	Step 1: The water is red. The flower is _____ .
_____	Step 2: The flower drinks the _____ and food dye.
_____	
_____	_____

I know about animal and plant needs.

Language lab 2

GRAMMAR 2: WE CAN / THEY CAN'T

I will describe actions using **We can / They can't.**

1 Look and write T (True) or F (False).

1 Ed and Rosie can't swim quickly. ☐

2 Zara and Dennis can swim quickly. ☐

3 Mark and Eva can run slowly. ☐

4 Sunil and Maisie can't run slowly. ☐

2 Correct the false sentences in 1.

1 _____   2 _____

3 🗨 Have a relay race.

MATHS ZONE

1 Play in four groups.

2 Groups run and hop for five metres.

3 Complete the table.

We can't run quickly, but Group 2 can run quickly.

	Group 1 time	Group 2 time	Group 3 time	Group 4 time
run				
hop				

4 Talk about the results.

4 Write about your relay race in 3.

Group I can run quickly. _____ _____

I can describe actions using We can / They can't .

My favourite animal

COMMUNICATION

I will describe my favourite animal.

1 031 **Look, listen and write.**

Ava   Ben   Ethan   Mia

2 **Play *Guess who*. Use the children in 1.**

Her favourite animal is a bird.

It's Ava!

Yes!

3 **Play *Draw and guess*.**

It's small. It's got two legs. It can fly …

Your favourite animal is a bird!

Yes! My favourite animal is a bird.

 describe my favourite animal.

PROJECT AND REVIEW UNIT 5

Choose the perfect class pet

1 Complete for your perfect class pet.

Our perfect class pet	
Is it big or small?	
What can it do?	
What does it eat?	

2 Complete your project report.

Our perfect class pet
Our perfect class pet is a rabbit. Its name is Hoppy. It can hop quickly. It's small and white. It eats plants and drinks water.

Our perfect class pet
Our perfect class pet is a _____ .
Its name is _____ .
It can _____
_____ .
It's _____ .
It eats _____ and drinks _____ .

3 Present your report to your family and friends.

This is our perfect class pet. Its name is Hoppy. It can hop quickly!

60

I can choose the perfect class pet.

4 Read, look and write. There are two extra animals.

1 It's small. It can run, but it can't swim. _hamster_

2 It can fly and it's got two legs. _____

3 It can hop and it's got big eyes. _____

4 It can hop and it can run quickly. _____

5 It can swim, but it can't fly. _____

6 It's small. It's got four legs and big ears. _____

7 It eats insects. It can climb, but it can't hop. _____

8 It's got four legs. It eats fish. _____

rabbit

lizard

hamster

horse

frog

mouse

fish

bird

cat

dog

5 Look at 4. Choose your favourite animal.

My favourite animal is the hamster.

6 Read and complete. Then write a clue for your partner.

It's small and brown.
It's got four legs.
It eats plants.
It can run and climb.
It's a _____ .

It's _____ .
It's got _____ .
It eats _____ .
It can _____ .
It's a _____ .

Now go to your Progress Chart on page 2.

6 Fruit bowl!

How can we make a fruit café?

1 🎧 032 Listen to the song. Write the number.

☐ mango   ☐ apples   ☐ oranges

2 Circle the odd one out. Then say.

3 Look at 2 and answer.

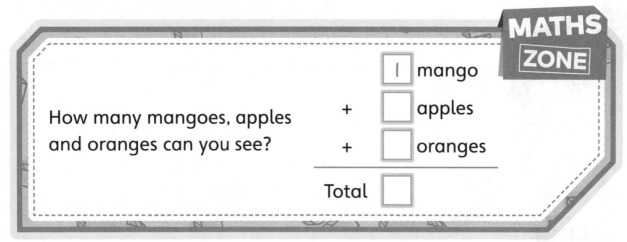

MATHS ZONE

How many mangoes, apples and oranges can you see?

1	mango
+ ☐	apples
+ ☐	oranges
Total ☐	

Lots of fruit

> I will learn fruit words.

1 Look and write.

1  (r a / e n o / g)

_____

2  (w i / i k)

_____

3  (i e / i a e / p l / n p p)

_____

4 (e r a / p)

_____

5  (a e / l / p p)

_____

6 (a n / n b a / a)

_____

7  (r l / t e n / m w o / e a)

_____

2 Match and draw.

5 strawberr	•	•	s
2 mango	•	•	ies
8 grape	•	•	es

EXTRA VOCABULARY

3 🎧 033 Complete. Then listen and repeat.

1   peach

2   plum

3   _____

4   papaya

5  _____

I can use fruit words.

Language lab 1

GRAMMAR 1: I / WE / THEY LIKE / DON'T LIKE

I will talk about what **we like** and **don't like**.

1 Read and match.

1 What do we like? •   • We like pears.

2 What do they like? •   • I like oranges.

3 What do you like? •   • They like mangoes.

2 Read and circle.

1 I like strawberries and / but I like watermelon.

2 We like bananas and / but we don't like grapes.

3 They don't like pears and / but they don't like apples.

4 You like kiwis and / but you don't like pineapples.

3 Read and write T (True) or F (False).

1 We like pears and watermelons. ☐

2 They like grapes, but they don't like bananas. ☐

3 We like mangoes, but we don't like pineapples. ☐

4 I don't like oranges, but I like apples. ☐

I can talk about what we like and don't like .

Story lab

Bird food

I will read a story about a fruit garden.

1 ⚙ **Make your story book.** ➡ **page 107**

1 Order and write the page numbers.

2 Complete the story.

3 Draw a cover.

4 Complete the story review.

2 💬 **Tick ☑ the fruit Sarah and Alexander like. Then ask and answer.**

What fruit do they like?

They like oranges, but they don't like kiwis.

3 **What's in Grandad's smoothie? Complete.**

A _____ .

A _____ .

An _____ .

I can read a story about a fruit garden.

Phonics lab

I will learn the l and r sounds.

1  **Look, listen and write l or r.**

Colour me!

1 ____emon   2 ____abbit   3 ____eaf   4 ____obot

2 Look and write the words. Then add more words.

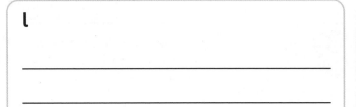 

l	r
_____	_____
_____	_____

3 Write the missing letters. Then say.

1 ____ucy's got long ____egs.   2 There's a ____abbit on the ____oad.

I can use the l and r sounds.

Experiment lab

I will learn about the life cycle of fruit.

1 Read and number.

CODE CRACKER

The flowers become fruit.

Trees grow from seeds.

There are seeds in the fruit.

Flowers grow on the tree.

EXPERIMENT TIME

Report

1 Complete the table.

1 seed	2–5 seeds	6–10 seeds	10+ seeds	Big seeds	Small seeds

2 Write your report.

How do we classify fruit seeds?
Results
There is one seed in the mango.
It's a big seed.
There are six seeds in the apple.
They are small seeds.

How do we classify fruit seeds?
Results
There _____
in the _____ .
_____
_____
_____

 about the life cycle of fruit.

Language lab 2

GRAMMAR 2: HE / SHE LIKES / DOESN'T LIKE

*I will talk about what **He / She likes** and **doesn't like**.*

1 Look, read and complete.

1   What _____ Phoebe like?

😋 She _____ kiwis, apples, grapes, strawberries and oranges.

☹ _____ bananas.

2   What does Simon _____ ?

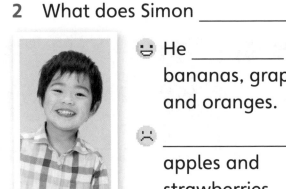

😋 He _____ kiwis, bananas, grapes and oranges.

☹ _____ apples and strawberries.

2 ⚙ Match the children in 1 to the fruit salads. Write Phoebe or Simon.

1 _____

2 _____

3 Follow and write about Tanya and Omar.

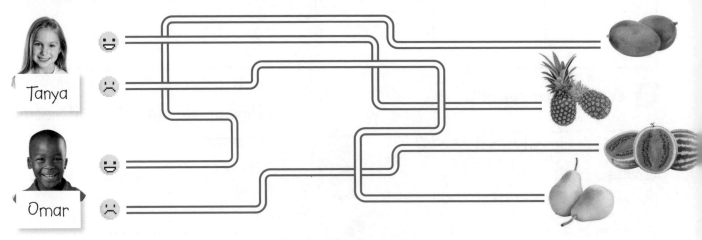

1   Tanya _____ , but she doesn't like _____ .

2   Omar _____ , but he _____ .

I can talk about what he / she likes and doesn't like .

Me too!

COMMUNICATION

I will learn how to agree with my friends.

1 Listen and draw 😃 or 😞 .

Ben and Madison

1  **2**  **3**  **4**  **5**  **6**

2 Ask and answer about the children in 1.

Ben and Madison don't like apples.

Me neither!

3 Play *Surprise box*.

What is it?

It's a train. I like trains.

Me too!

I can agree with my friends.

69

Make a class fruit café

Project report

1 Complete for your class fruit café.

Our class fruit café	
😃	🙁

2 Complete your project report.

Our class fruit café

In our café, we like kiwi and orange smoothies.
We like apple and mango ice lollies, too.
We don't like fruit salad.

Our class fruit café

In our café, we like

_____ .

We like _____

_____ , too.

_____

3 Present your report to your family and friends.

This is our class fruit café. We like kiwi and orange smoothies!

I can make a fruit café.

4 Read and write T (True) or F (False).

1 He likes bananas, but he doesn't like pears. ☐

2 He likes kiwis, but he doesn't like apples. ☐

3 She likes watermelons, but she doesn't like grapes. ☐

4 She likes strawberries, but she doesn't like mangoes. ☐

5 They like oranges, but they don't like pineapples. ☐

6 They like bananas, but they don't like watermelons. ☐

Jackson

Abigail

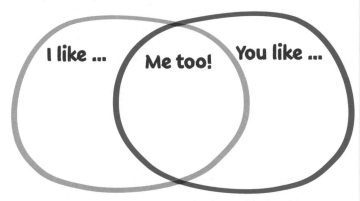

5 Correct the false sentences in 4.

6 Look and complete with your partner.

I like … Me too! You like …

Now go to your Progress Chart on page 2.

3 Checkpoint

1 Read and complete.

apple   dog   grapes   horse   kiwi   lizard   mango   mouse   orange   rabbit

Pets	
Fruit	

2 Draw a path.

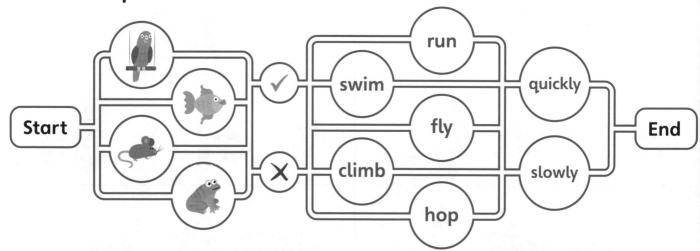

Start   run   swim   quickly   fly   climb   slowly   hop   End

3 Look at 2. Complete and draw.

1 What's this?

It's a _____ .

2 Can or can't?

It _____

_____

quickly / slowly .

4 Look, read and complete.

Pets

🙂 I like _____ .

🙁 I don't like _____ .

Fruit

🙂 I _____ .

🙁 I _____ .

Let's make a snake

CULTURE

1 Read and tick ☑ the correct sentences.

1 a The snake can climb quickly, but it can't run. ☐

b The snake can run quickly, but it can't climb. ☐

2 a The snail can swim quickly, but it can't climb. ☐

b The snail can climb slowly, but it can't run. ☐

3 a The elephant can climb slowly, but it can't run. ☐

b The elephant can swim quickly, but it can't climb. ☐

2 Look, match and write.

apples   bananas   elephants   mice   snails   snakes

1

_____

2

_____

They like _____.

They like _____.

3

_____

They like _____.

3 Ask and answer.

What do snails like?

They like apples.

How can we plan an activity day?

1 036 **Listen to the song. Tick ☑ or cross ☒.**

CODE CRACKER

swim	fly	hop	climb	play music	dance	sing

2 **What can you do? Tell your partner.**

I can't swim, but I can sing.

3 Look and complete.

1   I can _____ .

2   I can _____ .

3   I can

_____ .

I can dance!

I will learn hobbies.

1 Find and circle the hobby words.

1 r t d a n c e p

2 w y x s i n g l

3 q d r a w h m i

4 o i p a i n t k

5 y z e s w i m r

6 a e c l i m b o

2 Read and complete with play, read or ride.

1 _____ a book

2 _____ football

3 _____ a bike

4 _____ music

3   Look, listen and write. Circle the odd one out.

1 _____ a scooter

2 _____ a horse

3 _____ a board game

I can use hobby words.

Language lab 1

GRAMMAR 1: I / YOU / WE / THEY SWIM / DON'T SWIM

I will ask about hobbies using action words.

1 Order and write.

1 do? activities you What do

_____

2 but play music. I don't I sing,

_____

3 do What do? activities they

_____

4 draw, They don't they but paint.

_____

2 Ask and answer. Complete the tally table.

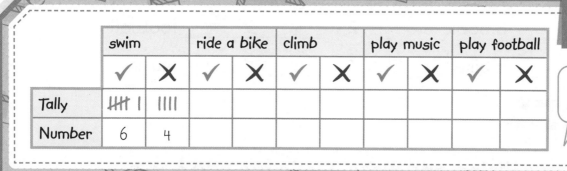

MATHS ZONE

	swim		ride a bike		climb		play music		play football	
	✓	✗	✓	✗	✓	✗	✓	✗	✓	✗
Tally	⳩⳩ I	IIII								
Number	6	4								

What activities do you do?

I play football, but I don't ride a bike.

3 Look at 2 and complete.

1 _____ students ride a bike, but _____ students don't _____

2 _____ students _____ , but _____ students _____

3 _____ students _____ , _____

 I can ask about hobbies using action words.

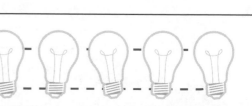

Story lab

> I will read a story about hobbies.

Circus School

1 Make your story book. → page 109

1 Order and write the page numbers.

2 Complete the story.

3 Draw a cover.

4 Complete the story review.

2 Read and circle T (True) or F (False).

1	I play football in the afternoon.	T / F
2	I dance in the afternoon.	T / F
3	I don't fly in the afternoon.	T / F
4	I don't climb trees in the afternoon.	T / F

3 Correct the false sentences in 2.

I don't _____ in the afternoon.

I _____ .

4 Look and write.

bike   tricycle   unicycle

1

2

_____   _____

3

_____

Phonics lab

I will learn the **h** and **w** sounds.

1 🎧 038 Look, listen and circle.

Colour me!

1   Harry is (hot / dot / not).

He's got a lot of (fair / hair / house).

He is wearing a (bat / hat / cat).

2   (We / He / I) are friends.

We (talk / walk / run).

We like (mangoes / apples / watermelons).

2 🎧 039 Listen and colour h words in blue. Colour w words in red.

3 Write words beginning with h or w.

h	w
_____	_____
_____	_____
_____	_____
_____	_____

I can use the **h** and **w** sounds.

Experiment lab

I will learn about the life cycle of a frog.

1 Look, number and write.

CODE CRACKER

frog   frog spawn   froglet   tadpoles

_____   _____   _____   _____

EXPERIMENT TIME

Report

1 Complete the table.

	Size of tail	Number of legs	Colour	Hop	Swim
eggs					
tadpoles					
froglets					
frog					

2 Complete the report.

The life cycle of a frog

1   My frog's eggs can't swim and they can't _____ . They're black.

2   Tadpoles can _____ , but they can't hop. They've got a big _____ .

3   _____ can swim, but they can't hop. They've got four _____ .

4   _____

 about the life cycle of a frog.

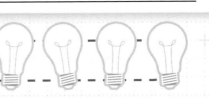

79

Language lab 2

GRAMMAR 2: HE / SHE SINGS / DOESN'T SING

I will ask about actions using **What does ...?**

1 Read and match.

1 What activities does he do? •

2 What activities do you do? •

3 What activities does she do? •

• She reads, but she doesn't draw.

• He sings, but he doesn't swim.

• We dance, but we don't climb.

2 Look and complete.

⚽ ✓	🎸 ✗
I _play football_ .	I _don't play music_ .
You _____ .	You _____ .
He _____ .	He _____ .
She _____ .	She _____ .
We _____ .	We _____ .
They _____ .	They _____ .

3  Ask and answer. Then circle and write.

What activities do you do?

I swim, but I don't play football.

What does my friend do?

He / She _____ , but he / she doesn't _____ .

He / She _____ , but he / she _____ .

I can ask about actions using What does ...?

When are you active?

COMMUNICATION

I will talk about the time of day.

1 🎧 040 **What does the girl do? Listen and tick ☑.**

1   2   3

2 💬 **Look and follow. Then ask and answer.**

Taj

What does Taj do in the morning?

He plays music in the morning.

3 ✴️ **Make an activity wheel. Then ask and answer.**

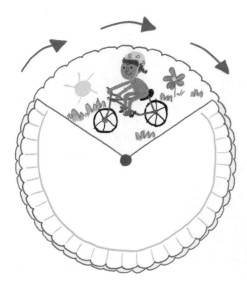

What do you do in the morning?

I ride a bike in the morning.

I can talk about the time of day.

81

Have an activity day!

Project report

1 Tick ☑ for your activity day.

dance ☐   read ☐   sing ☐   draw ☐   play football ☐

play music ☐   paint ☐   climb ☐   swim ☐   run ☐   hop ☐

2 Complete your project report.

Our activity day

At our activity day, we paint, dance and play music.
We don't play football and we don't swim.

Our activity day

At our activity day, we _____
_____
_____ .

We don't _____
_____
_____ .

3 Present your report to your family and friends.

At our activity day, we paint and dance. We play music, too!

I can have an activity day.

4 Read, look and number.

He climbs at the park. ☐

She rides a bike at the park. ☐

He plays football at the park. ☐

She reads at the park. ☐

He plays music at the park. ☐

She draws at the park. ☐

5 Read and write.

bird   fish   frog   lizard

1   It swims, but it doesn't fly.   _____

2   It sings, but it doesn't climb.   _____

3   It hops, but it doesn't run.   _____

4   It climbs, but it doesn't sing.   _____

6 Play *Mime and guess*.

Now go to your Progress Chart on page 2.

8 Let's dress up

How can I make a weather flap book?

1 Listen to the song. Then write a new verse and sing.

CODE CRACKER

bag   ball   book   bike

Find your _____ – it's red and blue.

Find your _____ , find your shoes,

Put on your shoes – shoe one, shoe two,

Pick up your _____ and your _____ , too.

2 Look and write.

feet   hat   head   shoes

1

2

3

4

_____   _____   _____   _____

3 Look and complete.

1

Put on your _____ .

2

Put on your _____ .

3

Put on your _____ .

Colourful clothes

VOCABULARY

1 Complete and say the alphabet.

A	B	C	___	E	F	G	H	I	___	K	L	M
■	✖	─	◗	●	⬠	★	❙	▲	◆	⬡	◢	⬠

N	O	___	Q	R	S	___	U	V	W	X	___	Z
↘	⬈	→	↓	←	↑	⬋	◇	◗	▶	✦	□	○

2 Use the code in 1 to write the words.

CODE CRACKER

1 ❙■⬋

_____

2 ─⬈■⬋

_____

3 ◗←●↑↑

_____

4 ↑❙⬈●↑

_____

5 ↑⬠▲←⬋

_____

6 ⬋←⬈◇↑●←↑

_____

EXTRA VOCABULARY

3 Look, listen and number. Use the code in 1 to write the words.

☐ ─■→

☐ ✖⬈⬈←↑

☐ ↑■◗◢■◢↑

_____ _____ _____

I can use clothes words.

Language lab 1

GRAMMAR 1: IN, ON AND UNDER

I will talk about where clothes are using **in**, **on** and **under**.

1 Look, read and complete.

in   on   under

1   The jumper is _____ the bag.

2   The socks are _____ the bag.

3   The jumper is _____ the bag.

2 Look, read and write.

1   The coat is on _____ .

2   The shoes are _____ .

3   _____ .

4   _____ .

3 Play *Remember the room*.

1   Look at the picture for one minute.

2   Cover the picture.

3   Tell your partner about the picture.

The doll is on the chair.

Yes! Well done.

I can say where clothes are using in , on and under .

Story lab

I will read a story about a pirate party.

Pirate Party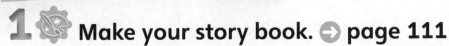

1 🌟 **Make your story book.** ➡ **page 111**

1 Order and write the page numbers.

2 Complete the story.

3 Draw a cover.

4 Complete the story review.

2 Circle Polly's costume in blue. Circle Sarah's costume in red.

3 Read and complete.

> big   coat   hat   small   trousers   T-shirt

1 Polly's got a _____ skirt.

2 Polly's got a small _____ .

3 Polly's got a blue and white _____ .

4 Sarah's got a red _____ .

5 Sarah's got a _____ hat.

6 Sarah's got brown _____ .

I can read a story about a pirate party.

Phonics lab

I will learn the **v** and **f** sounds.

1 Colour v blue **and** f red. **Then say.**

Colour me!

have   face   seven   five

2  **Look, listen and write the missing letters.**

1    The ____ish has a ____lower.

2    The ____ox has ____our ____eet.

3    The ____et has a ____an.

3 **Find and circle the words.**

o	k	f	e	v	a
f	l	o	w	e	r
i	m	x	p	t	s
s	z	i	d	y	u
h	b	v	a	n	g

I can use the **v** and **f** sounds.

Experiment lab

SCIENCE: THE WEATHER FORECAST

I will learn about the weather.

1 Look, read and complete.

snowy   sunny   windy

🌐 **WEATHER FORECAST**

In the morning	In the afternoon	In the evening

1 In the morning, it's _____ .

2 In the afternoon, it's _____ .

3 In the evening, it's _____ .

EXPERIMENT TIME

Report

1 Tick ✓ the weather today.

very windy ☐   windy ☐   not very windy ☐   not windy ☐

2 Complete your report.

The weather today

It's rainy and it's cold.
My windsock moves slowly.
It's not very windy.

The weather today

It's _____ and it's _____.
My windsock _____.

_____

I know about the weather.

Language lab 2

GRAMMAR 2: WHERE IS / WHERE ARE ...?

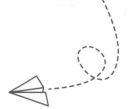
I can ask where clothes are using **Where ...?**

1 Read and circle.

1 Where **is** / are my umbrella?   It **is** / are in your bag.

2 Where is / **are** my gloves?   They is / **are** under the chair.

3 Where **is** / are your cap?   **It** / They is on your head!

4 Where is / **are** your boots?   It / **They** are in the car.

2 Read the questions and answers in 1. Then look and match.

3 Write questions. Then hide items for your partner to find.

My treasure hunt

Where are the crayons? Where is the ball?

_____

_____

_____

_____

Where is the ball?

It's in the hat!

I can ask where clothes are using Where ...?

What's the weather like?

COMMUNICATION

I will ask and answer about the weather.

1 Look, listen and number.

2 Make weather cards. Play *Snap!*

What's the weather like?

It's rainy!

Snap!

rainy

3 Look, read and circle. Then complete for today and say.

MATHS ZONE

1 It's (hot) / cold .   **2** It's (hot) / cold .   **3** It's _____ .

What's the weather like today?   It's hot.

I can ask and answer about the weather.

91

Make a weather flap book

Project report

1 Complete the table for your flap book.

	Weather 1: _____	Weather 2: _____
Clothes		

2 Complete your project report.

My weather flap book

It's hot.
She's got
shorts, a cap
and a T-shirt.
She's got socks
and shoes, too.

cap

T-shirt
shorts
socks
shoes

My weather flap book

_____
_____
_____
_____
_____
_____

3 Present your report to your family and friends.

This is my weather flap book. It's hot. She's got shorts! She's got a cap and a T-shirt, too!

I can make a weather flap book.

4 Look, read and tick ☑ the correct sentences.

1 a The ball is in the bag. ☐

  b The ball is under the bag. ☐

2 a The pencil case is on the purple book. ☐

  b The pencil case is under the pencil sharpener. ☐

3 a The hat is under the car. ☐

  b The hat is in the car. ☐

4 a The boy is on the book. ☐

  b The boy is under the book. ☐

5 Look at 4. Read and answer.

1 Where are the green shoes? _____

2 Where is the purple book? _____

3 Where is the black and white bag? _____

4 Where is the book? _____

6 Play *Hot or cold*.

Where is your book?

Cold ... cold ... hot!

It's under your jumper!

Yes!

1 Look and sort. Circle the words in the correct colour.

read   draw   on   dress   coat   cloudy
in   hot
under   cold
paint   sing   shorts   skirt   rainy

2 Draw a path.

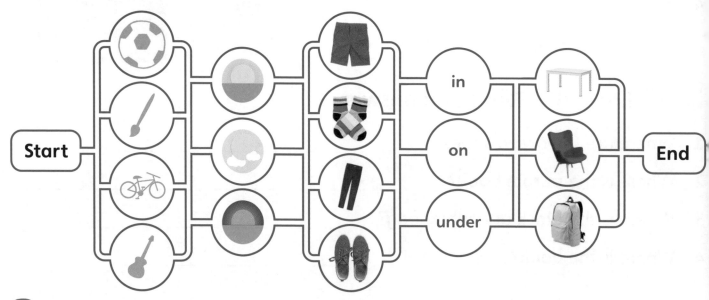

Start   End

in
on
under

3 Look at 2. Complete and draw.

1   What activities does he / she do?

He / She _____ .

2   When?

In the _____ .

3   Where are the clothes?

The _____ are in /
on / under the _____ .

94

Entertainment

CULTURE

1 🔅 **Circle the Bollywood costumes in red.**
Circle the Broadway costumes in blue.

2 Find and write the words. Then look at 1 and complete.

black   green   red   green

1   The Bollywood _____ is _____ .

2   The _____ is _____ and _____ .

3   The tap _____ are _____ .

3 💬 **Play Guess the show.**

It's Bollywood.

There are green hats.

Yes!

OUR WORLD

INTRO:
Here we stand: children of every age,
This is our world and the world's our stage.
We can laugh, we can cry — we can float, we can fly,
We can dance, we can sing — we can do almost anything
in OUR world ... our *beautiful* world.

VERSE 1:
Some of us are small; some of us are tall,
Some of us are shy; some say hi to everybody,
Some of us like numbers; some of us love words,
Some of us watch football, and some of us watch the birds!

(CHORUS)
This is our world ... we're different but the same.
We live and learn together — we get to know each other ...
in OUR world ... our *beautiful* world.

VERSE 2:
Some of us like music; some of us like cars,
Some of us draw pictures, looking at the stars,
Some of us are scientists, trying to find the code,
All of us can help a friend and give a hand to hold.

This is our world — there's room for everyone.
We learn to live together, and we have a lot of fun ...
In **our** world ... in **our** world ... in our beautiful world!

Unit 1

A story about toys.

Let's play together

It's an aeroplane!

It's a bus!

It's _____ !

No, no, no. It's _____ !

Hello! What's _____ ?

It's an aeroplane, a bus *and* a boat!

Hello! I'm Sarah. _____ Polly.

I'm Lee.

Hi! I'm Alexander. Let's play!

Hi! _____ Lily.

Characters

 Lily

 Lee

 Sarah

 Alexander

 Polly

My favourite character:

_____

My favourite story picture: ☐

No, no, no.
It's _____ !

No, no, no. _____
a boat!

What's this?

It's a _____.
Here.

_____ play together.

Unit 2

A **story** about a playhouse

A **rainbow** playhouse

Polly!

Look! Now _____ green paint!

The playhouse is _____ . Let's decorate it.

Good idea!

There are _____ and a glue stick.

Look at the _____ playhouse!

Well done, Polly!

_____ this?

_____ a playhouse.

Come in!

Characters

Lily

Lee

Sarah

Alexander

Polly

My favourite character:

_____

My favourite story picture: ☐

☆ ☆ ☆

What's _____ ?

It's a rainbow.

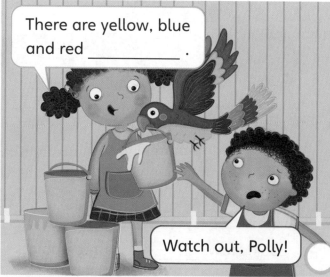

There are yellow, blue and red _____ .

Watch out, Polly!

Wow! There _____ toys and books.

There's orange paint and purple _____ , too.

Unit 3

A **STORY** about a family.

Characters

 Lily

 Lee

 Sarah

 Alexander

 Sofia

This is Lily and _____ Lee.

Nice to meet you!

Come to the party!

I know … let's have a party in the _____ !

This is my grandad.

_____ !

Nice to meet you. Please sit down.

My favourite character:

_____

My favourite story picture: ☐

Unit 4

A story about a monster.

It's a monster!

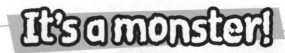

Stop! It's your _____ !

And it's your cousin Sofia and _____ teddy bear!

Look!

What a big shadow!

What happens next?
Read and draw.

Let's play with the toys!

Good idea.

_____ ?

This is my doll. Hello!

Characters

Lily

Lee

Sarah

Alexander

Sofia

Uncle

My favourite character:
_____

My favourite story picture: ☐

It _____ three heads!

_____'s got six arms!

It's got big ears!

Help! _____ a monster!

This is _____ .
Nice to meet you!

Shh! Listen!

Hello! _____
I play?

_____ ,
Sofia!

What a big _____ !

Unit 5

A story about a hat.

My hat can hop!

Look! It's a _____ !

Sarah, _____ hat can swim!

My _____ animal is a bird.

_____ favourite animal is a _____ . Bye, Frog!

Look at _____ hat!

_____ can hop!

Characters

Lily

Lee

Sarah

Alexander

Polly

My favourite character:

_____

My favourite story picture: ☐

_____ a magic hat!

Watch out, Polly! You _____ swim!

My hat can fly!

Come on!

Look! It can _____ !

My hat _____ hop, climb or swim …

… _____ the frog *can* hop, climb and swim!

And Polly can fly!

Unit 6

A story about a fruit garden.

Bird food

Now I've got a mango, _____ banana, and _____ orange.

Look!

I _____ pineapples.

_____ , but look … I've got four bananas!

Here – a banana, _____ and orange smoothie for you. And a _____ salad for the birds!

Mmm! It's delicious. _____ !

This is my garden. _____ fruit do you like?

Let's make fruit _____ !

We like oranges and mangoes, _____ we don't like kiwis.

Characters

Grandad

Sarah

Alexander

Polly

My favourite character:

_____

My favourite story picture: ☐

Mmm, I _____ bananas!

Sarah! Now _____ 've got three bananas.

_____ make smoothies!

_____ out!

I _____ oranges.

_____ . Look, I've got six oranges and two mangoes.

Look at Polly and her friends! _____ don't like bird food ...

... but _____ like fruit!

Unit 7

A story about hobbies.

Circus School

I _____ through the air!

Wow! I _____ circus school.

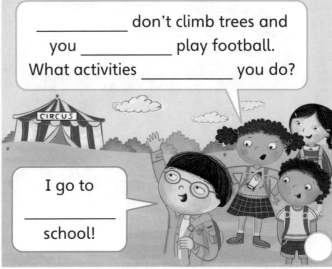

_____ don't climb trees and you _____ play football. What activities _____ you do?

I go to _____ school!

This is _____ teacher, Mr Chuckles.

Welcome to Circus _____ !

_____ , Mr Chuckles!

Let's _____ !

_____ , I don't play football in the _____ .

Characters

Alexander

Sarah

Lee

Lily

Mr Chuckles

My favourite character:

_____

My favourite story picture: ☐

☆ ☆ ☆

Look! I _____ climb!

Wow! You can climb _____ , Lee!

Look! I _____ , too!

You're _____ !

Let's _____ trees!

No, _____ don't climb _____ in the afternoon.

I _____ a unicycle!

Watch out!

Unit 8

A story about a pirate party.

Pirate Party

Sarah, your _____ is small!

Your _____ is small!

And your _____ is small!

The skirt is _____ the _____ .

Thank you!

Now we _____ all ready. Let's go to the _____ !

Wait, Sarah! Tie _____ shoelaces!

It's _____ pirate party _____ !

I like your pirate _____ , Lily. My pirate clothes are in my _____ .

Characters

Alexander Sarah

Lee Lily Polly

My favourite character:

_____

My favourite story picture: ☐

☆ ☆ ☆

The T-shirt is _____ the _____ .

Thank you!

The hat is _____ the _____ .

_____ you!

Look at your _____ , Sarah! Watch out!

Ahh! _____ bag!

This _____ my costume.
This _____ Polly's costume!
My _____ is in my bag.

Unit 1

Creativity

Critical Thinking

Coding

Communication

Unit 2

Creativity

Critical Thinking

Coding

Communication

Unit 3

Creativity

Critical Thinking

Coding

Communication

Unit 4

Creativity

Critical Thinking

Coding

Communication

Unit 5

Creativity — Critical Thinking — Coding — Communication

Unit 6

Creativity — Critical Thinking — Coding — Communication

Unit 7

Creativity — Critical Thinking — Coding — Communication

Unit 8

Creativity — Critical Thinking — Coding — Communication